BOLD & EASY COLORIN

HALLOWEEN

RiRi Luvs Crayons

Reminder: If using markers, please put a protective sheet behind the page you are coloring so it doesn't bleed through to the other pages. Happy Coloring!

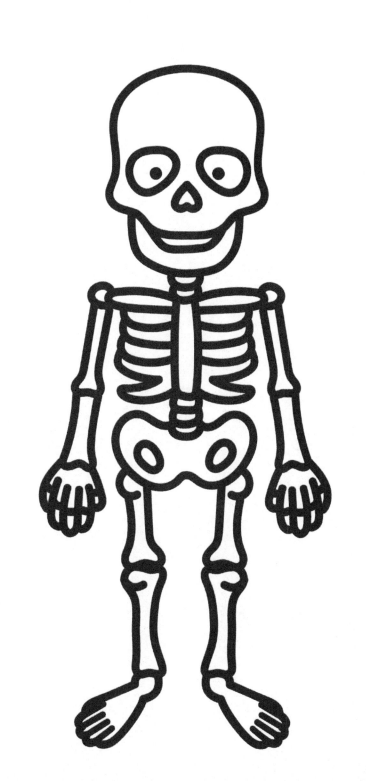

CHOCOLATE

Peanut Butter

CARAMEL

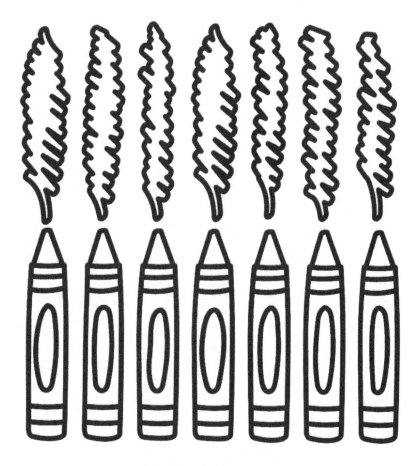

@ririluvscrayons

Fall is one of my favorite times of the year. Where I live the leaves change color, the morning air is crisp, cider mills are bustling and the pumpkins are ready for picking and carving. All leading up to Halloween – the costumes, parties and trick-or-treating! This coloring book (my 7th one) captures all these wonderful moments of the season and holiday. I hope you have a great day and don't forget to stop by my social media channels to say Hi! Happy Halloween!

Happy coloring,
RiRi

Made in the USA
Las Vegas, NV
22 August 2024

94264949R00037